D1240095

T.R.

TR

CHAMPION OF THE

Theodore Roosevelt Association   *New York*

STRENUOUS LIFE

A Photographic Biography
of Theodore Roosevelt

By WILLIAM DAVISON JOHNSTON

Copyright © 1958 by William D. Johnston
Library of Congress Catalog Card Number: 58-14286
Seventh Printing, 1991

Typography and layout: Barbara Fay Johnston

Manufactured in the United States of America

ACKNOWLEDGMENTS

An expression of appreciation is due to all those who have assisted in this work, particularly to the Theodore Roosevelt Association and to its Director, Mr. Leslie Stratton, and to Miss Mae Manning, and Miss Helen MacLachlan; to the Harvard College Library and to the Curator of the Theodore Roosevelt Collection, Mr. Robert Haynes, and to his assistant, Miss Audrey Hosford; to Theodore Roosevelt's daughter, Mrs. Richard Derby, and to his daughter-in-law, Mrs. Theodore Roosevelt; to Mrs. Richard Kimball of the American Museum of Natural History; Mrs. Jessica Kraft, Curator of Sagamore Hill; Mrs. George McFadden; and to Mr. Hermann Hagedorn, Chairman of the Theodore Roosevelt Centennial Commission. My deepest gratitude is reserved for my wife for her constant encouragement and assistance, and especially for her page designs for the entire book.

To David Johnston

About the
Theodore Roosevelt Association...

TR: Champion of the Strenuous Life by William Davison Johnston is published by the Theodore Roosevelt Association. The Theodore Roosevelt Association, founded in 1919, was chartered by a special Act of Congress in 1920 "to perpetuate the memory of Theodore Roosevelt for the benefit of the people of the United States of America and the world." The TR Association is a nonprofit national historical society and public service organization.

"For the benefit of the people of the United States of America and the world," the Theodore Roosevelt Association reconstructed the Theodore Roosevelt Birthplace, 28 East 20th Street, New York City, in 1923; in 1931 purchased an island in the Potomac River, and named it "Theodore Roosevelt Island" as a memorial to TR in the nation's capital; and opened TR's Oyster Bay, Long Island home, Sagamore Hill, to the public in 1953. The Association gave all three sites to the National Park Service, U.S. Department of the Interior. In 1943 the Association donated the Theodore Roosevelt Collection, consisting of over 12,000 books, 10,000 photographs, 3,500 cartoons, and thousands of manuscripts and letters, to the Harvard College Library. The TRA today maintains a purchase fund for additions to the TR Collection. The TRA also donated a large film archive on Roosevelt and his times to the Library of Congress. In 1960 the TRA founded the Theodore Roosevelt Memorial Fund at the American Museum of Natural History. The fund provides research grants for natural history on an annual basis, and continues to receive financial support from the Association.

Through the years, the TRA has published many books on Theodore Roosevelt, and provided research assistance to historians, the media, and the general public. The Association regularly sponsors lectures, student contests and awards, and many other programs to promote TR's ideals and spread knowledge of his life and career. The Association publishes a quarterly magazine, *The Theodore Roosevelt Association Journal,* and works in close cooperation with sites dedicated to TR all over the nation.

Membership in the Association is open to all interested in perpetuating the memory of Theodore Roosevelt. For information about the TRA, and a free copy of the *Journal,* write to the THEODORE ROOSEVELT ASSOCIATION, P.O. BOX 720, OYSTER BAY, NEW YORK 11771; or phone 516-922-1221.

CONTENTS

INTRODUCTION

This is the story of a man who studied to be a scientist and rose to the Presidency; who, though remembered as a statesman, thought of himself as a writer and historian; an adventurer and explorer, the intimate of cowboys and kings, the champion of the strenuous life.

The Theodore Roosevelt that is pictured in history books and biographies as a soldier and politician is but a fragment of the real man. He was more than a distinguished public figure. His endless interests, his omnivorous reading, his outstanding accomplishments in so many fields of human endeavor, added to his well-known record in public service, make him, like Benjamin Franklin, one of the most versatile and interesting Americans.

This book is an attempt to re-create the many facets of his remarkable life. T.R. did so much, said so much, had such an astounding abundance of creative energy that no single medium would suffice to portray the man as he appeared to his countrymen a half century ago. The principal events of his career are revealed in the historic photographs collected here, many for the first time. These photographs, some torn and cracked, portray not only Roosevelt's tumultuous life, but also record the forward march of a people, the maturing of a great nation.

But though the photographs show the encyclopedic nature of his interests, it is only through his writings and speeches that we come to understand the kind of man Theodore Roosevelt was. His warm personality, his wisdom, his courage, his dedication—all are revealed in his own striking phrases. Whether addressing a great audience on a national issue, or describing a hunting trip to his children, T.R. said much that is timeless, and in a way that made many of his writings a part of our literature and his sayings a part of our language.

Above all, Theodore Roosevelt is worth remembering because he spent himself generously in the great adventure of life. Worldly, but simple in heart, terrible in battle but generous and understanding, he lived the full life in joyous fashion. Individualistic, uninhibited and audacious, he left an example of all that is admired and cherished in a free man.

WILLIAM DAVISON JOHNSTON

THE STRENUOUS LIFE

"...I wish to preach, not the doctrine of ignoble ease, but the doctrine of the strenuous life, the life of toil and effort, of labor and strife; to preach that highest form of success which comes, not to the man who desires mere easy peace, but to the man who does not shrink from danger, from hardship, or from bitter toil, and who out of these wins the splendid ultimate triumph."

THEODORE ROOSEVELT

I

THE EARLY

YEARS

"Character, in the long run, is the decisive factor in the life of an individual . . ."

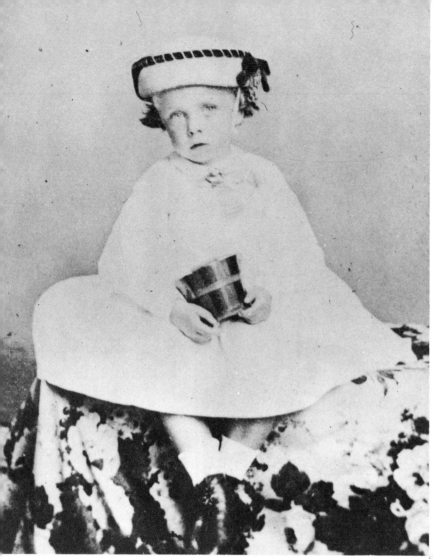

Theodore Roosevelt as a child of eighteen months.

Roosevelt's birthplace, now a museum.

CHILDHOOD

"On October 27, 1858, I was born at 28 East 20th Street, New York City. . . . My father was the best man I ever knew. . . . My mother, Martha Bulloch, was a sweet, gracious, beautiful Southern woman, a delightful companion and beloved by everybody."

Theodore Roosevelt, statesman, explorer, author, scientist, and twenty-sixth President of the United States, was the eldest son of a wealthy and distinguished New York family. Emigrating from Holland in 1644, his ancestors had lived on Manhattan Island for seven generations and had been active in the early history of the Republic, serving in the Army and the Continental Congress. His father, a successful glass merchant, was one of the city's foremost citizens and a founder of the American Museum of Natural History. During the Civil War, when Theodore was very young, the family was divided politically, with his mother loyal to the South and his father, a friend of Lincoln, strong for the Union cause. In spite of the stress and anguish of their times, Theodore's parents transmitted to their children their own warmth and vitality, wide interests and a rare zest for life.

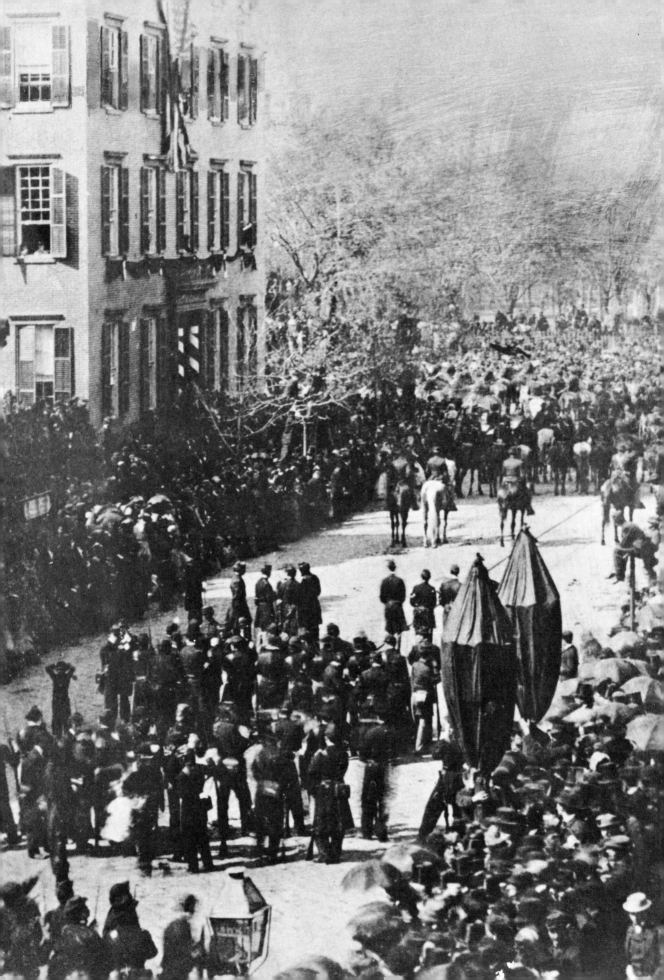

FAMILY BACKGROUND

"Now and then we children were taken round to our grandfather's house; a big house for the New York of those days, on the corner of Fourteenth Street and Broadway, fronting Union Square."

Theodore Roosevelt grew up in the midst of historic times and events. The drama of the nation's struggle for survival was all about him: the rumble of wagons and the tramp of troops off to the battlefields of Virginia and Pennsylvania; the years of despair when the Federal armies marched only to defeat; the bloody draft riots, convulsing New York City for days, killing and injuring thousands and bringing the metropolis to the verge of martial law; the tragic funeral of the murdered President, the avenues draped in black, the long, solemn procession, viewed by the Roosevelt children from the window of their grandfather's house, as it passed up Broadway. Theodore, just seven years old, too young even to dream of being President, would himself one day be inaugurated to that high office, wearing on his hand a ring containing a lock of hair from the brow of Abraham Lincoln.

17

Lincoln's funeral passing the Roosevelt house. One of the children visible in the upper window is believed to be Theodore Roosevelt.

BOYHOOD

"I remember distinctly the first day I started on my career as a zoologist. I was walking up Broadway, and as I passed the market. . . I suddenly saw a dead seal laid out on a slab of wood. That seal filled me with every possible feeling of romance and adventure."

Even as a young boy "Teedie," as his family called him, was intensely interested in all things out-of-doors. Birds and animals delighted him and at ten he began systematically to record his observations in a nature diary. The "Roosevelt Museum of Natural History," started when he was hardly out of the nursery, was begun with the skeleton head of a seal and was a typical small boy's collection of shells, insects, minerals and birds' nests. Taxidermy lessons, a new shotgun, and a leisurely family trip up the Nile in 1872 were all that was needed for the start of a genuine nature collection. While his brothers and sisters viewed the ruins of Egypt, Theodore made inroads into the bird population of the Nile Valley. From this trip alone he brought back about two hundred specimens. Several examples of his work, including the Snowy Owl, are still beautifully preserved in museums throughout the country.

"die," the budding naturalist, at age ten.

A Snowy Owl, collected and mounted by Theodore Roosevelt in 1876, now in the Museum of Natural History.

Theodore Roosevelt at seven

YOUTH

"... while, thanks to my father and mother, I had a very happy childhood I am inclined to look back at it with some wonder that I should have come out of it as well as I have!"

Although, as a youth, Theodore had the advantages of a well-to-do and happy home, repeated attacks of asthma left him frail and sickly. He was too ill to attend school regularly and received all of his early education from tutors. Confined to the house, he read books of adventure and outdoor life which fired his imagination. With a determination rare in one so young, he strove to overcome his physical weakness. Boxing lessons, exercise in his indoor gym, and family trips to the Adirondacks built his strength toward the robust manhood that years later would enable him to swim the wintry waters of Washington's Rock Creek Park, or face a lion's charge in the African jungle. The greatest improvement came during the happy summers at Oyster Bay where he swam and rode with his friends and romped over the grassy knoll on which he would someday build his home and call it Sagamore Hill.

COLLEGE

"No man has a right to arrogate to himself one particle of superiority or consideration because he has had a college education, but . . . it makes it doubly incumbent upon him to do well and nobly in his life. . . ."

When Roosevelt entered Harvard in 1876 his ambition was to become a field naturalist like Audubon or Baird. He found that classroom emphasis was on the microscopic study of cells, and decided, midway through college, to give up his plans for a career in science. Expanding his interests, he grew enthusiastic about history, literature and politics. But Roosevelt, although an honor student, was not one to limit his enjoyment to one side of any undertaking, and became a first-rate boxer, a sporting driver of a dog cart, and a sociable, party-going good fellow who wore sideburns and fashionable clothes. Somehow the spark of self-reliance and originality had been kindled, for, in his last year at the university, without consulting his professors, he wrote the first chapters of his well-known history, *The Naval War of 1812.*

...eady for a boxing match at Harvard.

The young Assemblyman with some of his friends from the New York State Legislature.

An election poster from his first campaign.

21st Assembly District.

40th to 86th STS.,   **LEXINGTON to 7th AVES**

We cordially recommend the voters of the TWENTY-FIRST ASSEM[BLY] District to cast their ballots for

THEODORE ROOSEVELT

FOR MEMBER OF ASSEMBLY.

and take much pleasure in testifying to our appreciation of his high character standing in the community. He is conspicuous for his honesty and integrity, eminently qualified to represent the District in the Assembly.

NEW YORK, November 1st, 1881.

F. A. P. BARNARD,	EDWARD MITCHELL.
WILLIAM T. BLACK,	WILLIAM F. MORGAN,
WILLARD BULLARD,	CHAS. S. ROBINSON,
JOSEPH H. CHOATE,	ELIHU ROOT.
WM. A. DARLING,	JACKSON S. SCHULTZ.
HENRY E. DAVIES.	ELLIOTT F. SHEPARD.
THEODORE W. DWIGHT,	GUSTAVUS TUCKERMAN.
JACOB HESS,	S. H. WALES,
MORRIS K. JESUP,	W. H. WEBB.

BEGINNINGS IN POLITICS

"You can't govern yourselves by sitting in your studies and thinking how good you are. You've got to fight all you know how, and you'll find a lot of able men willing to fight you."

During his last year in college, Roosevelt decided to enter politics, and when he arrived home joined the local Republican Club in spite of the advice of friends that politics was a dirty business. In 1881 he ran for the New York State Legislature from Manhattan's wealthy silk-stocking district and was overwhelmingly elected. The three terms he spent in Albany were an education in practical politics and a fighting challenge to correct the abuses he found. Lacking in experience but not in courage, he went before the Legislature to demand the impeachment of a judge of his own party. Although derided and threatened by organization leadership, the vigor and persistence of his attacks attracted public attention and an investigation was held. The professionals for the first time took notice of the freshman who had ability, conviction, and a knack for attracting attention to any cause he espoused.

FRONTIERSMAN

"It was still the Wild West in those days, the Far West, the West of Owen Wister's stories and Frederic Remington's drawings, the West of the Indian and the buffalo-hunter, the soldier and the cow-puncher. . . . In that land we led a free and hardy life, with horse and with rifle. . . . Ours was the glory of work, and the joy of living."

The young Assemblyman's future looked bright. He had a beautiful young wife, a small cattle ranch in the Dakota Territory, and a promising career in the New York State Legislature. He had received a large inheritance from his father and plans were completed for a handsome country home at Oyster Bay. But his good fortune was not to continue, for the death of his wife and mother on the same day caused him to abandon the East and return to his ranch in the wilderness. For two years he lived the life of a frontiersman and cowboy, learning to throw a lasso, brand a steer, and live from dawn to dusk in the saddle. He experienced the hardships and dangers of Western life—fighting and disarming a drunken desperado, riding furiously through a stormy night to break up a stampede. The West of 1885, which only nine years before had witnessed the slaughter of Custer and his men, was still the "Wild West" and Roosevelt became a part of the American frontier.

Roosevelt as a cowboy in the Dakota Territory.

CHIMNEY BUTTE RANCH.
THEODORE ROOSEVELT, Proprietor.
FERRIS & MERRIFIELD, Managers.

P. O. address, Little Missouri, D. T. Range, Little Missouri, 8 miles south of railroad.

as in cut on left hip and right side, both or either, and down cut dewlap.
Horse brand, on left hip.

With Sewall and Dow, ranch hands who helped capture the boat thieves.

ELKHORN RANCH.
THEODORE ROOSEVELT, Proprietor.
SEAWALL & DOW, Managers.

P. O. address, Little Missouri, D. T. Range, Little Missouri, twenty-five miles north of railroad.

as in cut, on left side, on right, or the reverse.
Horse brand, on right or left shoulder.

Cattle brands used on the Roosevelt ranches.

RANCHER

"All daring and courage, all iron endurance of misfortune, . . . make for a finer and nobler type of manhood."

Roosevelt enjoyed the strenuous work, the hardy companions, the stark beauty of the Bad Lands. The young "four-eyes" from the East was no longer regarded as a curiosity and earned a reputation for courage and hardihood which his capture of some boat thieves helped to enhance. When Roosevelt discovered, one wintry morning, that his river boat had been stolen he lost no time starting in hot pursuit. Undiscouraged by the prospect of a chase down the ice-choked river, he helped build and launch another boat. After three days on the river, Roosevelt and his two companions surprised and captured the thieves at their camp. Three hundred miles and another week of bitter cold and hunger passed before their prisoners were turned over to the law. To Roosevelt, now "brown and tough as a hickory nut," came an understanding of the West, its struggling settlers, its Indians and outlaws—one possessed by few men born east of the Mississippi.

CANDIDATE FOR MAYOR

"But anyway, I had a bully time."

The years at the Elkhorn Ranch did not spell isolation for Theodore Roosevelt, for between occasional trips East and his lively correspondence he kept remarkably well informed of political developments. Recognized as an important, though youthful, political leader he had led the New York delegation to the Republican National Convention in Chicago. Now, after his years at the ranch, he returned home to run for Mayor against Tammany and Henry George. He went into the race with his usual energy and enthusiasm knowing, however, that it was "a perfectly hopeless contest." It is difficult to believe that T.R., a candidate for Mayor of New York, was but twenty-eight years old.

An election cartoon from the New York World, *1886. Roosevelt, the Republi« "cowboy," and Henry George trying to stop the Tammany machine.*

The young candidate for Mayor of New York City.

MARRIAGE

"There is no other such happiness on earth as there is for a true lover, and a sweet, fair girl beloved."

A few days after losing the election the young widower surprised his friends by leaving for London to marry Edith Carow, his childhood playmate. Edith, demure and pretty, was his sister Corinne's closest friend and she and Theodore had been fond of each other since they first met in grandfather Roosevelt's house years before. She, too, had been one of the carefree young people at Oyster Bay, and when Theodore brought his bride back to Sagamore Hill the happy childhood memories were still fresh in their minds. Edith shared her husband's love of the rolling hills and sparkling bay as well as his fondness for books, for children and for people. Here she, also, would lead a busy life, raising six spirited children, running a twenty-three-room house, and—not the least of her accomplishments—tempering T.R.'s ebullient spirit with her own calm judgment.

Edith Carow at the time of her marriage to Theodore Roosevelt.

II

THE EMERGING

GIANT

"...I rose like a rocket."

A popular view of the Commissioner's victory over the spoils system.

CIVIL SERVICE COMMISSIONER

". . . when my duty is to enforce the law, that law is surely going to be enforced. . . . I am perfectly willing to be turned out—or legislated out —but while in I mean business."

For a time he concentrated on writing his famous history, *The Winning of the West,* but Theodore Roosevelt could not keep out of the hurly-burly of public office and managed to obtain an appointment to the United States Civil Service Commission. It was an insignificant post and paid but $3,500 a year, yet Roosevelt saw its potentiality. His report of blackmail in the U. S. Customs House in New York was the beginning of a long series of disclosures revealing the evils of the sordid patronage system. Outraged by campaign assessment of Federal job holders, he declared that "offices are not the property of the politicians at all . . . on the contrary, they belong to the people and should be filled only with regard to the needs of public service." Such sentiments brought from spoilsmen of both parties insistent demands for his removal. But Roosevelt, who was reappointed during a Democratic administration, loved a fight, and returned every attack, blow for blow. When he left Washington after his "six years' war," 26,000 more jobs were no longer political plunder.

FAMILY LIFE

"For unflagging interest and enjoyment, a household of children, if things go reasonably well, certainly makes all other forms of success and achievement lose their importance by comparison."

T.R., intensely occupied in politics, in writing, and in pursuing a host of other interests, was never too busy to be a delightful father to his children, or to take an active part in family affairs. Warm, affectionate, possessor of an abundant good nature, he made his home and family the center of his activities. Although there were many demands on his time, he could somehow manage a frolic with his children or a quiet row on the bay with Mrs. Roosevelt. Even during his most active years he still found a moment to play "bears" in the gun room, or read to the youngest boys and girls before tucking them into bed. The Roosevelt family, photographed when T.R. was Civil Service Commissioner, was recalled by his children as an exceedingly lively and happy household.

The Roosevelt family in 1894.

POLICE COMMISSIONER

"Be practical as well as generous in your ideals. Keep your eyes on the stars, but remember to keep your feet on the ground."

By now Roosevelt was nationally known—his name synonymous with honesty and reform. It was not surprising therefore, when Mayor Strong, swept into office on a reform ticket, asked Roosevelt to be Commissioner of Police. His acceptance marked the beginning of the modern police force which New York boasts today. Finding it a demoralized and corrupt political pawn he modeled the police along military lines, into a genuine law-enforcing agency. Meritorious work was rewarded, standards of admittance and training were improved, and the cop on the beat and the precinct captain were kept alert by the possibility that the vigorous Commissioner might appear on an inspection trip at any hour of the day or night. On these trips Roosevelt, often accompanied by his friend Jacob Riis, gained his familiarity with the social problems to be found on the streets, in the tenements, and in the police courts of the country's largest city.

T.R. in his office at Police Headquarters on Mulberry Street.

T.R. and the children playing football on the lawn at Sagamore

CHILDREN'S COMPANION

"There could be no healthier and pleasanter place in which to bring up children than in that nook of old-time America around Sagamore Hill."

Theodore Roosevelt's enjoyment of children was immediate and unaffected. By some wonderful alchemy, he retained a youthful outlook that enabled him to see the world through a child's eyes. Father of four boys and two girls, and "Cousin Theodore" to a score of their playmates, he often was the ringleader in the strenuous games around the big house and the old barn. One of his particular inventions was the overland obstacle race through briar, pond, and haystack, ending in a precipitous slide down a sand bank, known as Cooper's Bluff. The children and T.R. would return amid uproarious laughter, wet and begrimed, but vowing they had never had such fun. Roosevelt shared his imaginative and adventurous spirit with children in a way that endeared him to them always. When his youngest son, on a special occasion, received a new rifle too late in the evening to be tested out-of-doors, father and son took the treasure upstairs, and fired the first shot into the ceiling.

ASSISTANT SECRETARY OF THE NAVY

Washington, February 25, 1898

Dewey, Hong Kong:

Order the squadron, except the Monocacy, to Hong Kong. Keep full of coal. In the event of declaration of war Spain, your duty will be to see that the Spanish squadron does not leave the Asiatic coast, and then offensive operations in Philippine Islands. Keep Olympia until further orders.

Roosevelt

Appointed Assistant Secretary of the Navy on the eve of the Spanish-American War, Roosevelt did his utmost to put the fleet into battle readiness. Ships were purchased and armed, coaling stations established at strategic ports around the world, and gunnery practice was stepped up. With his tremendous drive and infectious enthusiasm, much of the credit belongs to Roosevelt for converting the peacetime Navy into an efficient fighting machine. His audacious cable to Admiral Dewey, sent over a weekend while he was Acting Secretary, would make possible the smashing victory of the American Squadron over the Spanish Fleet at Manila Bay. When all hope of peace had vanished with the sinking of the U.S. Battleship *Maine* in Havana Harbor, the Navy was ready.

44

The Assistant Secretary at his desk in front of a model of the Olympia.

Colonel Theodore Roosevelt of the Rough Riders.

ROUGH RIDER

"All—Easterners and Westerners, Northerners and Southerners, officers and men, cowboys and college graduates, wherever they came from, and whatever their social position—possessed in common the traits of hardihood and a thirst for adventure."

Shortly after war was declared, Roosevelt, feeling that his work with the Navy had been completed, sought a command in the Army for its invasion of Cuba. Having advocated war with Spain he now believed it his duty to take an active part in the fighting. He was commissioned by the President as Lieutenant Colonel of the First United States Volunteer Cavalry, a regiment which soon became known as the Rough Riders. Composed of men from every part of the country, its all-American character caught the public imagination. Among the troopers were Dudley Dean, star Harvard quarterback, Bucky O'Neil, famous Apache-fighter and Arizona sheriff, and Hamilton Fish, captain of the Columbia crew. Indians, sportsmen, gold prospectors, Texas Rangers and New York Police—all were part of the colorful regiment of horsemen. It was a time of high adventure, but for Roosevelt, whose wife and small son were severely ill at Oyster Bay, it was also a time of great anxiety.

"To the right the jungle was quite thick . . . and the Mauser bullets were singing through the trees over our heads, making a noise like the humming of telephone-wires. . . ."

A bare two months of whirlwind training were allowed Colonels Wood and Roosevelt to whip their irregulars into shape. The Rough Riders embarked from Tampa, Florida, where all was a welter of confusion. Only the quick wits of T.R., who managed to commandeer a transport assigned to another regiment, prevented the Rough Riders from being left behind. The American Expeditionary Force effected a landing on the Cuban mainland without opposition and began a march toward Santiago to contact the main Spanish army. The Rough Riders had a brief but hot engagement at Las Guasimas and this was followed by an even fiercer fight at San Juan Hill in which Roosevelt led the charge on horseback. The next day the nation rang with news of the American victory and of the gallant leadership of Teddy Roosevelt.

48

COLONEL OF THE REGIMENT

The Command Staff of the American Expeditionary Force confers at the jungle's edge. Colonel Roosevelt is in the foreground, second from the right.

Roosevelt and a group of his men after they disembarked at Montauk Point, Long Island.

WAR HERO

"To keep us here, in the opinion of every officer commanding a division or a brigade, will simply involve the destruction of thousands. There is no possible reason for not shipping practically the entire command North at once."

Letter to Major General Shafter
August 3, 1898

Overnight the Colonel of the Rough Riders became the symbol of the typical American fighting man and to his surprise he found himself a national hero. Now the war was over. After only four months the crushing victory over Spain was complete. Nevertheless the War Department wanted the Army to stay in Cuba although it was in danger of being wiped out by an epidemic of malarial fever. Roosevelt's reaction was typical—he released to reporters a copy of a letter he had written to General Shafter citing medical authority that the Army would perish if it remained in the mosquito-infested jungle any longer. The press and public opinion did the rest. Orders were issued from Washington for the immediate return of the troops. Complete disaster had been averted from an army that had already suffered more casualties from malaria than from battles. However, Roosevelt, who had jogged the military authorities into action, never received the Medal of Honor for which he had been recommended.

GOVERNOR OF THE EMPIRE STATE

"In popular government results worth having can only be achieved by men who combine worthy ideals with practical good sense...."

When the Army disembarked at Montauk Point, Roosevelt found that he was being considered as a candidate for the governorship of New York. Revelations of the misuse of Erie Canal funds made re-election of the Republican incumbents doubtful, and although the Rough Rider reformer was not the choice of Boss Platt, a popular hero was needed to keep the party in office. In a campaign novel for its vigor, he criss-crossed the state speaking at every village and whistle stop. Colonel Roosevelt, thanks to his war record and appealing personality, was able to win by a narrow margin. T.R. in office proved to be an astute politician as well as an able administrator, free from the domination of Boss Platt. Seizing the initiative, he strengthened the laws regulating sweatshops and tenement housing, and tightened the supervision of utilities and insurance companies. Changes long overdue in food and drug handling, hours of labor, and the employment of women and children made his administration one the voters of the state and Thomas Platt would remember.

53

The Roosevelt campaign train pauses at Cattaraugus, New York, in 1898.

CHAMPION OF THE STRENUOUS LIFE

"We hold work not as a curse but as a blessing, and we regard the idler with scornful pity."

Theodore Roosevelt possessed robust health, an unusually able intellect, and an incredible amount of physical and mental energy. He firmly believed that life should be lived to the full, that a man should spend himself in endless striving after great things. His devotion to this ideal, which he called "the strenuous life," accounts in some measure for his astonishing creativity in so many diverse fields. He hated idleness, and found relaxation in changing from one activity to another. In the course of a single day, he could box for an hour, deliver a political address, write a magazine article, spend several hours at his desk attending to the duties of public office, and find time to have a pillow fight with the children. One can only marvel that he was able to keep up this pace, not on isolated occasions but every day of the year.

Keeping the woods cleared near Sagamore Hill was considered sport, not work, by T.R.

Writing in his study at Sagamore Hill.

Protected from insects by headnet and gauntlets Roosevelt writes in the Amazon wilderness.

AUTHOR

"I have written the first chapter of the Benton; so at any rate I have made a start. Writing is horribly hard work to me; and I make slow progress."

Roosevelt not only lived a many-sided, vigorous life but he also produced writings which in quality and quantity would do credit to a first-rank author. His reputation as a writer had preceded his prominence as a public figure, for he had published a score of works before becoming Governor. Twenty-eight books, countless essays and articles, and 150,000 letters reflect his many interests and constitute a truly prodigious output. A considerable portion of his work was done under adverse conditions and Roosevelt could turn out the daily chapters of a book amid swarms of insects in the jungle, or in his comfortable study at Sagamore Hill. Of all that he has written, the letters most truly reveal the man; his sparkling sense of humor, his capacity for friendship, his tendency to assail those who disagreed with his point of view. He wrote to statesmen and to cowboys, but most often to his family, particularly his own children. The volume of *Theodore Roosevelt's Letters to His Children* with his delightful drawings is something of a minor classic in American literature.

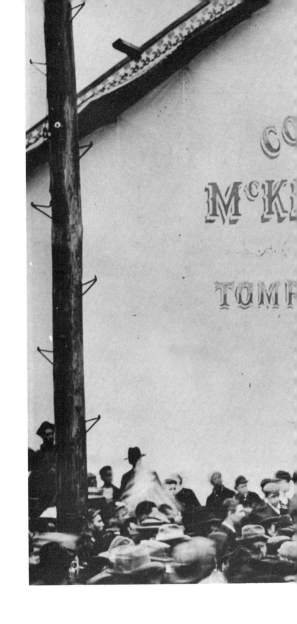

VICE-PRESIDENT

"If I have been put on the shelf, my enemies will find that I can make it a cheerful place of abode."

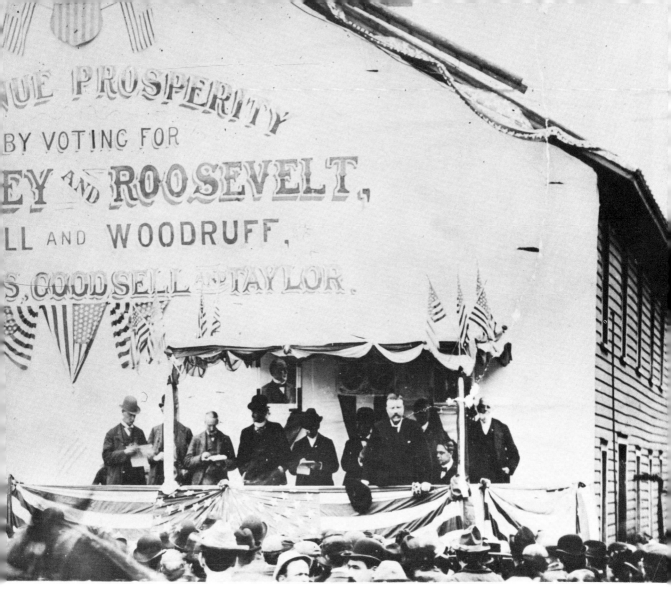

The Vice-Presidential candidate at an outdoor rally at the Ramapo Iron Works, Hillburn, New York, 1901.

As the year 1900 approached, there was a great deal of talk about nominating Theodore Roosevelt for Vice-President on the Republican ticket. Support for Roosevelt by the delegates of the convention was spontaneous and enthusiastic. Boss Platt was no less enthusiastic and there was good reason to believe that Platt had carefully made his plans to get the reform Governor off his hands by burying him in the Vice-Presidency. Roosevelt, fully aware of what Platt was up to, could not stem the popular tide for his nomination. McKinley and Roosevelt were swept into office on Election Day. Six months after his inauguration, President McKinley was shot in Buffalo and died after a few days. Roosevelt, summoned from the slopes of Mt. Marcy in the Adirondacks to the bedside of the dying President, arrived only in time to be sworn in as the youngest President in the history of the Republic.

III

PRESIDENT OI

THE UNITED STATES

"We are face to face with our destiny and we must meet it with a high and resolute courage."

THE NEW CENTURY

"Much has been given us, and much will rightfully be expected from us. . . . We have become a great nation, forced by the fact of its greatness into relations with the other nations of the earth, and we must behave as beseems a people with such responsibilities."

America at the dawn of the Twentieth Century was coming of age. Heir to Spain's island possessions, it found that the ancient policy of isolation was no longer tenable. Under the terms of the peace treaty, the United States had assumed a protectorate over Cuba, and also had acquired complete title to the islands of Puerto Rico, the Philippines, and Guam. The nation had grave responsibilities in its new world role. It also had serious domestic problems. The uncontrolled growth of great corporations and the frequent exploitation of American wage earners was about to result in the formation of trade unions and in a series of industrial conflicts between management and labor. It was under these challenging conditions that Theodore Roosevelt, in his forty-second year, became the nation's Chief Executive. He brought to the Presidency imagination, ability, and an originality not seen since Lincoln.

*new President speaking at Nahant, Massachusetts. His close friend,
...tor Henry Cabot Lodge, sits at the left, high hat in hand.*

SOCIAL REFORMER

"No man can be a good citizen unless he has a wage more than suffi-cient to cover the bare cost of living, and hours of labor short enough . . . to bear his share in the management of the community. . . ."

In the year 1901, the strength of the Populist and Free Silver movements and the agitation of the Socialists bespoke the deep unrest in American life. Depressed farm prices, poor factory working conditions, and the sixty-hour week heightened the tensions. The difference between wealth and poverty was extreme. While Andrew Carnegie in 1900 made $23,000,000 tax free from his steel business, the average American took home less than five hundred dollars. Up to this point, only the cries of the injured had been heard, but now it was the voice of the President which spoke for social justice. Here was a man of wealth, position and unquestioned loyalty to democratic principles, who insisted that the problems of the industrial era would have to be faced, and that every citizen was entitled to a "square deal." In settling the great coal strike of 1902, he demonstrated his matured respect for the laboring man.

65

eeting the blacksmith-Mayor of Texline, Texas.

AT SAGAMORE HILL

Roosevelt's devotion to Sagamore Hill was natural, for it was filled with the associations of the past; with his own childhood, and with his family life, which he cherished. Its crest, where Indian tribes had met three hundred years ago, was still an inspiring place to live, and Theodore Roosevelt was a man with the perception and sensitivity to enjoy its beauty. He swam, rode horseback, and listened to the Long Island songbirds. During the summers when he was President, it became the nation's White House. Many a crucial decision was made in the library with cabinet member or foreign diplomat. Often a conversation of world import was held over the single primitive telephone in the pantry. Sagamore Hill still echoes with the turbulent life of this strenuous American and his happy family.

"At Sagamore Hill we love a great many things—birds and trees and books, and all things beautiful, and horses and rifles and children and hard work and the joy of life."

The Roosevelts of Sagamore Hill go for a morning ride

The President cooking over an outdoor fire.

"Father" ready for a camping trip.

FATHER

"Stand the gaff, play fair; be a good man to camp out with."

T.R. always remained an engaging father and friend to his children. He believed in treating young people like adults, allowing them to form their own judgments and opinions. Seldom did he give orders; always it was his warm suggestions that the children hastened to obey. Activities changed as the Roosevelt children grew older, but their father's participation and interest remained constant. Overnight camping trips were regular diversions during the summer, baffling to the Secret Service men who found that the President had slipped away in a rowboat for a night's trip to a distant beach. After a supper of beefsteak and pan bread cooked by T.R., the children huddled around the roaring fire as darkness fell, and listened to their father's endless fund of stories of Indians and wild animals, of hero tales from history, of life on the plains and mountains. When the fire died down and they wrapped themselves in their blankets, there was always a final ghost story, and as T.R. reached the fearful climax, he would suddenly sieze one of his listeners amid the screams of delight and terror of the entire group.

TRUST-BUSTER

"We are today suffering from the tyranny of minorities. It is a small minority that is grabbing our coal deposits, our water power . . . that lies behind our monopolies and trusts."

Congress, perceiving the swollen power of certain monopolistic combines, and the threat they posed to the free enterprise system, had in 1890 passed the Sherman Anti-Trust Act. Bravely conceived, the law had lain on the shelf, the only test case having been dismissed by the Supreme Court five years later. When J. P. Morgan and his associates formed the Northern Securities Company to merge the railroads, thus monopolizing transportation in the Northwest, they never suspected the trust law would be enforced. But they failed to reckon with the new President. Roosevelt's plans to prosecute the Northern Securities trust were kept secret, and the news of the court action burst like a thunderbolt on men that T.R. characterized as "malefactors of great wealth." Morgan was outraged, and rushed to Washington to see the President. "The whole thing is simply a misunderstanding," he stormed. "We can easily compromise the matter." President Roosevelt's reply was decisive: "There can be no compromise in the enforcement of the law." Although Roosevelt's efforts to regulate big business met with heavy opposition, the principle of government action to protect the public interest was firmly established.

T.R. attacks the trusts in a speech at Providence, R.I.

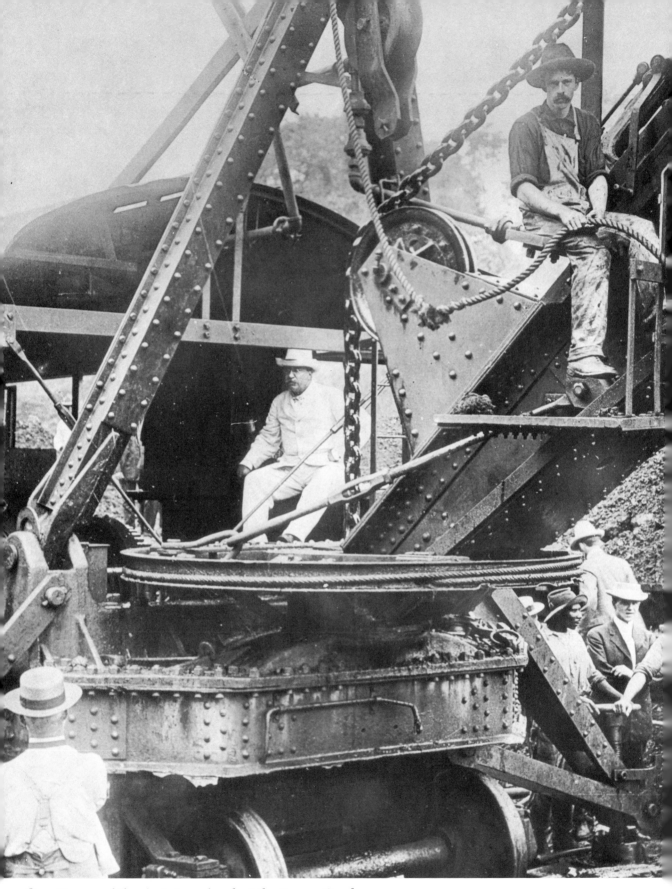

Operating one of the giant steam shovels at the Panama Canal.

CANAL BUILDER

". . . I took the Isthmus, started the canal, and then left Congress— not to debate the canal, but to debate me . . . . But while the debate goes on the canal does too; and they are welcome to debate me as long as they wish, provided that we can go on with the canal."

To Theodore Roosevelt more than any other man must go the credit or blame for building the Panama Canal. When, after years of negotiations, the Colombian Government balked at the terms for leasing a strip across the Isthmus, a revolution began in the province of Panama. Roosevelt's immediate formal recognition of the insurgent government secured the canal rights for the United States. As he anticipated, the debate over the propriety of his action is still going on. The qualities of the men appointed to supervise the enormous engineering and health problems were to a large degree responsible for their successful solution. Colonel Goethals, in charge of the construction, and Dr. William Gorgas, who conquered the mosquito and yellow fever in the Isthmus, were men chosen by the President. While many are critical of the manner in which the canal rights were acquired, few are unwilling to accept the canal as a prime factor in the growth of the United States as a world power, and as one of the main props to its foreign policy.

The Submarine Plunger *on which Roosevelt made his voyage under the Sound.*

ENTHUSIAST

"No President has ever enjoyed himself as much as I...."

If T.R. had a dominant characteristic, it was his boundless enthusiasm. To Roosevelt there was no such thing as the commonplace, and he managed to live on a high plateau of excitement. Greeting crowds, or inspecting the newly invented submarine, could be events of genuine pleasure for the youthful President. Roosevelt's visit to the new submarine, the U.S.S. *Plunger,* took place on a dark and rainy day when he was at Sagamore Hill. The bay was covered with whitecaps, and the rain came in heavy squalls when the President, in oilskins, bounded out of a steam launch onto the narrow deck of the undersea craft, and stepped smartly down the ladder to the control room. In a few minutes the sixty-foot cigar-like craft with its seven-man crew was cutting its way into the rough water of the Sound. For nearly three hours the sub dove and resurfaced with the delighted President assisting at the controls. T.R.'s day was complete when Lieutenant Nelson, the sub's commander, turned out the lights thirty feet below the surface and demonstrated how the craft could be operated in complete darkness. "I've had many a splendid day's fun in my life," said T.R. as he left the *Plunger,* "but I can't remember ever having crowded so much of it into such a few hours."

74

The President greeting crowds near St. Louis on a Mississippi River trip

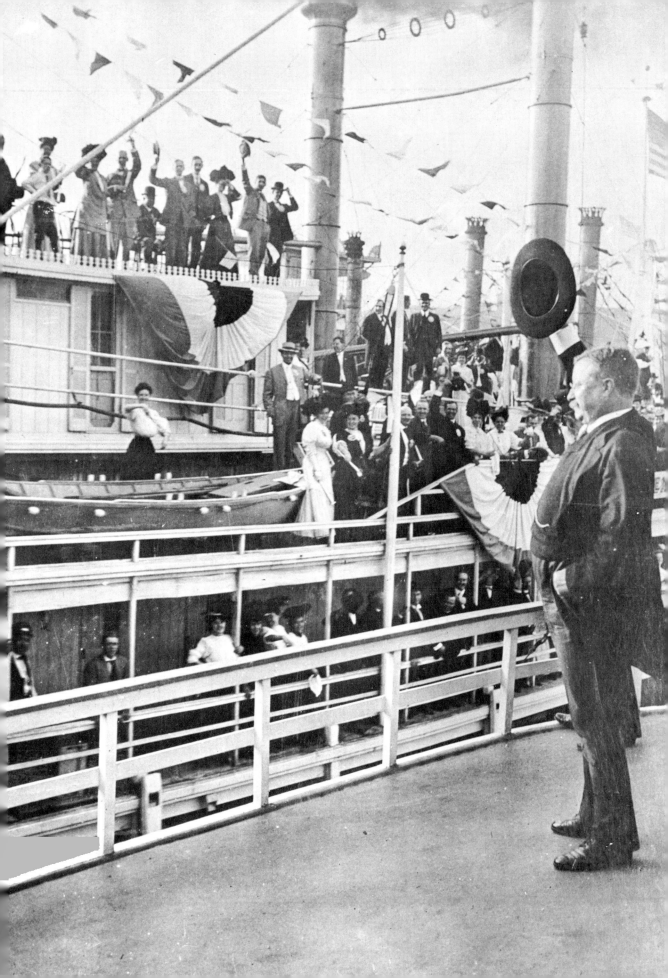

*At the Roosevelt camp on the Red River, Colorado. The President,
the first man on the right, stands with his horse.*

Roosevelt's vacations, unlike those of other Presidents, were
spent hunting or camping. To him a holiday meant an expedition after panthers in Colorado, a winter camping trip in a
national park, or a wolf hunt in Oklahoma. Such colorful
activities made lively reading, and the reporters and cartoonists
had a heyday. It was on one such occasion, a bear hunt in
November 1902, that the famous cartoon of T.R. and an appealing young bear was published, and resulted in the creation
of the Teddy Bear. On this trip the newspapermen got wind
of the fact that the President, in search of grizzlies, had refused to shoot a small bear that some members of the party
had captured; furthermore, he had insisted on turning the cub
loose. Berryman of the *Washington Post* saw the article and
drew the cartoon. Little did he imagine that toy-makers across
the country would seize upon the idea and that thereafter the
Teddy Bear would find a place in every nursery.

OUTDOORSMAN

"The morning of the first day of our hunt dawned bright and beautiful, the air just cool enough to be pleasant."

RE-ELECTION, 1904

"We, here in America, hold in our hands the hope of the world, the fate of the coming years; and shame and disgrace will be ours if in our eyes the light of high resolve is dimmed, if we trail in the dust the golden hopes of men."

As his first term drew to a close, Theodore Roosevelt had grave doubts of his chances for re-election. He had displeased a large majority of machine politicians by his independence, and had held labor leaders to strict account where lawless violence was involved. Worst of all, he had dealt rough blows to the financial supporters of the party, the big corporations, and they could be counted on to work actively for his defeat. But if his policies had alienated certain elements, they had won the enthusiastic support of the great majority of plain citizens. Running against a comparative unknown, Judge Parker, a conservative Democrat, T.R. scored a landslide victory, receiving the largest majority and the greatest plurality ever before given a candidate. The inaugural parade was one of the most colorful on record, with troops from the Philippines and Puerto Rico, cowboys and Indians from the Western plains, and of course the Colonel's own beloved Rough Riders. Not since ante-bellum days had Washington seen an inauguration in which range riders and backwoodsmen played such a prominent part, or cheered a President who represented the choice of so many diverse elements of American society.

Theodore Roosevelt delivering his inaugural address, March 1905.

PEACEMAKER

"It would be a master stroke if those great powers honestly bent on peace would form a League of Peace, not only to keep the peace among themselves, but to prevent, by force if necessary, its being broken by others."

Nobel Prize Speech—May 1910

The two terms of the Roosevelt administration were years of peace and international prestige for the United States. Strangely enough, T. R. is better remembered for his combativeness than for his willingness to compromise, and for his talent in settling disputes. Roosevelt, the man the cartoonists portrayed with the big stick, was the first to use the Hague Tribunal in a dispute with Mexico. He was also awarded the Nobel Peace Prize for his arbitration of the Russo-Japanese War in 1905. In the settlement of this war not only did his personal messages to the Emperor of each country bring about the initial talks but, when the conference seemed likely to fail, he suggested the terms of concession that resulted in the Treaty of Portsmouth. In his speech accepting the Nobel Prize in Christiania, Roosevelt clearly foresaw the central idea later embodied in the United Nations.

Roosevelt meets with the peace envoys aboard the presidential yacht, Mayflower, to end the Russo-Japanese War.

THE BIG STICK

FOR CERTAIN PARTIES

Archie Roosevelt ready for a ride around the White House.

Never had the Presidency been so enjoyed as by T.R. Never had the staid old White House seen such a family as his. Hardly had the six strenuous, uninhibited children moved in before they cut loose. They rode bicycles and roller skates on the hardwood floors, and crawled in the air spaces between ceilings and floors where no one had ventured since the house had been built. Every member of the family (except the President and Mrs. Roosevelt) had a pair of wooden stilts, and no stair was too well carpeted nor too steep to block the clomping cavalcade. The ushers and servants, used to the musuem-like quiet, were completely overwhelmed by the riotous games, but the elders acted as if it were all quite normal, and T.R. himself frequently participated. Eventually Quentin's pony going up in the elevator, baseball games in the South Garden, or a dip by the younger boys in the fountain were accepted as customary. Enormous popular interest attended the brilliant wedding of T.R.'s daughter, "Princess" Alice, to Representative Longworth in the East Room at high noon before 700 guests.

82

WHITE HOUSE GANG

November 19, 1905

Dear Kermit,

. . . One afternoon . . . Archie turning up with his entire football team . . . we had obstacle races, hide-and-go-seek, blind man's buff, and everything else; and there were times when I felt that there was a perfect shoal of small boys bursting in every direction, up and down stairs, and through and over every conceivable object.

Your loving father,
T. R.

Two members of the gang line up with the White House police.

In an era that produced William Jennings Bryan and Woodrow Wilson, Theodore Roosevelt's stirring speeches made some of the most memorable scenes in American political history. To hear Roosevelt, in his well-modulated, sometimes staccato voice, discuss the issues of his time was an unforgettable experience to millions of Americans. The newsmen's cameras have faithfully recorded the gleaming teeth, the dramatic gestures, the rapt attention of his audience. But almost legend is the fire in his voice, the occasional high-pitched falsetto echoing far out over the crowd, the impact of his magnetism and sincerity. Using his office as a pulpit, Theodore Roosevelt preached the strenuous life, the need for personal excellence, the duties of citizenship, and the responsibilities of freedom. In a rich Harvard accent, touched with a bit of New York and more than a trace of the Western plains, he filled a generation with a vision of what America might become.

PUBLIC SPEAKER

". . . go back to your homes and your daily lives with a resolute purpose to war for honesty in its deepest and broadest significance both in our business and in our politics. . . ."

Waiting for T.R. at Freeport, Illinois.

". . . this country will not be a permanently good place for any of us to live in unless we make it a reasonably good place for all of us to live in."

Evanston, Illinois

PUBLIC SPEAKER

"Americanism is a question of spirit, conviction, and purpose, not of creed or birthplace."

San Francisco

Asheville, North Carolina

"The things that will destroy America are prosperity-at-any-price, peace-at-any-price, safety first instead of duty first, the love of soft living, and the get-rich-quick theory of life."

BOOK LOVER

"There are men who love out-of-doors who yet never open a book; and other men who love books but to whom the great book of nature is a sealed volume...."

Roosevelt's love of books was as fundamental as his love of people or ideas, and he always had a book with him wherever he went. He enjoyed the world of thought and the moments between the larger tasks were spent reading. Roosevelt's tastes in books paralleled his wide interests. The classics, contemporary novels, science and philosophy, short stories, and politics were among his favorites. He probably read as much poetry as he did history, and his befriending of the young poet Edwin Arlington Robinson by an appointment to a Federal job allowed the poet to continue his writing. Roosevelt read with remarkable speed, two or three books a day, retaining much of what he had read in his extraordinary memory. With no desire to be labeled an intellectual by his political opponents, Roosevelt managed to conceal the extent of his cultural pursuits. The voters who sent him back to the White House in 1904 probably never knew that their President could produce a copy of Homer or Huxley as readily in the jungle as he could in his study in the White House.

The President of the United States and a friend at the West Divide Creek ranch house.

The American battlefleet returning from its voyage around the world.

BUILDER OF THE NAVY

"Speak softly and carry a big stick."

It was a memorable day for the United States Navy when the Great White Fleet steamed past the presidential yacht into Hampton Roads after its circumnavigation of the globe. It was also a proud day for President Theodore Roosevelt who had planned the long voyage to demonstrate the power and efficiency of the American Navy. Roosevelt believed that naval strength was the key to national survival and the only basis for an effective foreign policy. When Germany had announced its intention of occupying Venezuela to collect debts overdue, Roosevelt, invoking the Monroe Doctrine, informed the Kaiser that Dewey and the fleet would prevent the invasion. The Kaiser decided to arbitrate and trouble was averted. As a tribute to Theodore Roosevelt, his birthday is celebrated as "Navy Day."

CONSERVATIONIST

"I recognize the right and duty of this generation to develop and use the natural resources of our land; but I do not recognize the right to waste them, or to rob, by wasteful use, the generations that come after us."

Roosevelt's historic efforts to preserve America's unmatched natural wealth and beauty from exploitation and ruin is perhaps his great legacy to its people. By the end of the nineteenth century more than half of the nation's priceless timber had been cut, vast quantities of topsoil had been washed into the rivers and many species of wild life faced extinction. It was fortunate at this juncture that a natural scientist of T.R.'s caliber and training became President. Against powerful opposition he set aside 150 million acres of forest timberland, over fifty wild game preserves, and doubled the number of national parks. Of the sixteen national monuments he established, best known is the Grand Canyon of Arizona. Even a critical biographer has called his conservation program "great forward-looking statesmanship."

T.R. and John Muir, the naturalist, riding out of the valley at Yosemite.

LEADER

"...we need leaders of inspired idealism, leaders to whom are granted great visions, who dream greatly and strive to make their dreams come true; who can kindle the people with the fire from their own burning souls."

Convinced that a strong Chief Executive was essential to the American form of government, Roosevelt undertook to establish a precedent for leadership. He felt that the President should formulate policy, and then mobilize public opinion to secure its approval. His philosophy of the presidency was in the tradition of Lincoln and Jackson. "I believe it should be a very powerful office," he said, "and I think the President should be a very strong man who uses without hesitation every power that the position yields." Coming into office at a time of peace and on the heels of an administration opposing change, he made the first decade of the twentieth century one of the nation's most exciting and fruitful eras. Whatever his final place in history, Theodore Roosevelt already stands with that company of great leaders who have given new direction and vitality to American life.

95

sident Theodore Roosevelt in his study in the White House.

IV

THE MANY-SIDEI

ROOSEVELT

*"The joy of living is his who has
the heart to demand it."*

AFRICAN HUNTER

"There are no words that can tell the hidden spirit of the wilderness, that can reveal its mystery, its melancholy, and its charm. There is delight in the hardy life of the open, in long rides rifle in hand, in the thrill of the fight with dangerous game."

Roosevelt with Captain Slatter a few moments after killing the rhino.

As Roosevelt's term drew to a close, having declined re-nomination, he enthusiastically planned a trip to Africa. Sponsored by the Smithsonian Institution, it would turn out to be the most successful scientific expedition ever made to the Dark Continent. Less than a month after leaving office, and with nine pairs of spectacles in his pack, he plunged into the bush at Mombasa, not to emerge until eleven months later at Khartoum on the Upper Nile. It was a strange sight for the natives of the Congo and the Sudan, this giant safari, led by a bushman carrying the American flag, with Roosevelt, Kermit, and the naturalists on horseback, and two hundred porters stretched out far behind. T.R. and Kermit did the shooting, while museum experts prepared the thousands of skins of every species, including lions, pythons, pygmy mice, elephants, hartebeests, and honey birds. The charge of a black rhinoceros in the Wakamba country was one of the hunter's unforgettable moments, for Roosevelt had to fire both barrels of his powerful Holland rifle to bring the raging beast to a stop only thirteen paces from his feet.

99

Delivering the Romanes Lecture at Oxf[...]

SCHOLAR

"The historian should never forget, what the highest type of scientific man is always teaching us to remember, that willingness to admit ignorance is a prime factor in developing wisdom out of knowledge."

From the Romanes Lecture

Roosevelt's original plans for his African trip had not included a European visit, but he changed his mind when he received an invitation to deliver the Romanes Lecture at Oxford. It was a high honor for an American to be invited to speak where Gladstone and Huxley had lectured before him. Combining his expert knowledge of history and natural science, he spoke on "Biological Analogies in History," tracing the parallel development of intelligence in the animal world and in man. He could have discoursed as readily on ancient Irish sagas, the Mongol conquests, and the exploits of Boleslav the Glorious. For Roosevelt was as much a scholar by nature and training as he was a man of action. The technique of research and study developed in preparing his early historical works became such a habit in his daily reading that he was still able to maintain an astonishing fund of new knowledge even in his more crowded years. The learned societies, such as the American Academy of Arts and Letters, had early recognized Roosevelt's scholarship by electing him to membership, and in 1912 he became president of the American Historical Association. The major universities of Europe saluted his outstanding ability by awarding him their highest honors.

EUROPEAN TRAVELER

When it was learned that Theodore Roosevelt planned to visit Europe the reigning heads of state vied with each other for his attendance at their courts. He went to Paris and spoke to the gowned dignitaries of the Sorbonne as well as the highest ministers in the government. He saw the Kaiser, reviewed the German Army, and prophetically observed the seeds of the coming world conflict. Similar visits were made to the Netherlands, Hungary, and Italy; and finally, as official American representative, he attended the funeral of Edward VII of England. The kings and princes of Europe were much impressed by the charm and democratic demeanor of the man whom they regarded as a typical American. His interest in sports and big-game hunting was shared by these monarchs, but he noted that most were bored with the restrictions of their station. Their surprise at his intimate knowledge of their national literature and history amused him. Characteristically, however, he regarded as most precious those moments he spent with Lord Grey in the Valley of the Itchen, identifying English songbirds.

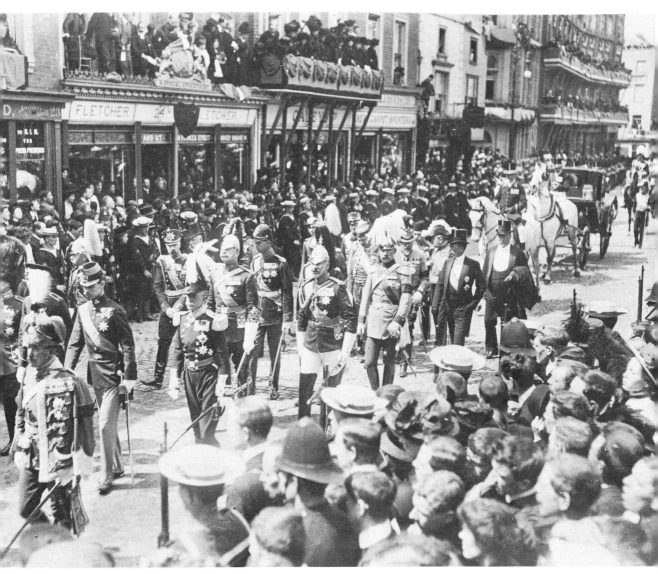

America's special envoy walks in the rear of the procession of kings at the funeral of Edward VII.

"...the king's lack of political power, and his exalted social position, alike cut him off from all real comradeship with the men who really do the things that count...."

"I do not greatly care for the reproduction of land-scapes which, in effect, I see whenever I ride or walk, I wish 'the light that never was on land or sea' in the pictures that I am to live with."

In the Museum at Versailles.

Private citizen Roosevelt and Kaiser Wilhelm review the German Army.

"I had rather hoped to find myself mistaken about him, but I found his point of view very sordid."

EUROPEAN TRAVELER

Rough Riders in the welcoming parade.

HOMECOMING

". . . I am more glad than I can say to get home, to be back in my own country, back among the people I love."

Roosevelt going up the harbor on a cutter. T.R.'s young cousin, Franklin D. Roosevelt, stands on the deck at far right.

The tumultuous welcome which T.R. received on his return to America after his fifteen-months' absence has seldom been exceeded, even in a later age of channel swimmers, trans-Atlantic fliers, and victorious generals. As his ship steamed into New York harbor that hazy June morning, it was met by six flag-bedecked battleships and innumerable destroyers, pleasure boats and harbor craft. The forts and naval vessels fired a twenty-one-gun salute as he transferred to the government cutter which took him to the Battery. A sea of humanity met Roosevelt at the dock, and cabinet members and New York politicians and city fathers were treated to his firm handshake and exuberant greeting. A giant parade followed to City Hall, and then up Fifth Avenue to 59th Street, with flags and bands and Rough Riders and Spanish War veterans marching through the cheering crowds. As T.R. joyfully joined his family at Sagamore Hill with the adulation still ringing in his ears, he had almost forgotten his dread of returning to the "cauldron of politics" that had been brewing in his absence.

A walk with a friend.

FRIEND

*"He was the prism through which the light of day took on more colors
than could be seen in anybody else's company."*

Said of Theodore Roosevelt
by his friend William Hard

An extrovert by nature, Theodore Roosevelt was well endowed to be a warm and affectionate friend to a variety of men. As a man of many interests, he had formed lifelong friendships with people all over the world. Among his favorites were "Bat" Masterson, John Burroughs, Buffalo Bill, Rudyard Kipling, Augustus Saint-Gaudens, "Battling" Nelson, Sir George Trevelyan, and John Hay, to name but a few. Some came frequently to Oyster Bay to discuss every subject under the sun, taking the slow steam train from New York and then the three-mile carriage ride from the station to Cove Neck. Others, especially when he was in Washington, dropped in during his daily exercise period and found themselves engaged in a battle with broadswords, or a round of medicine ball. Nearly all corresponded with him regularly. Holding interests in common with a diversity of men, he filled all of them with his own ebullient spirit and enthusiasm. One of his friends likened him to radium, that infuses all about it with its fire. Another, the writer Julian Street, explained that Theodore Roosevelt "possessed a certain vital force which everyone near him felt, but no one could define."

AERONAUT

NAVY DEPARTMENT

WASHINGTON
March 25, 1898

Sir:

Mr. Walcott, Director of the Geological Survey, has just . . . shown me some interesting photographs of Professor Langley's flying machine. The machine has worked. It seems to me worthwhile for this government to try whether it will not work on a large enough scale to be of use in the event of war. . . .

T. Roosevelt
Assistant Secretary

Preparing to go aloft in Hoxsey's airplane, St. Louis, 1910.

T.R. was not only the first President to fly—he was also one of the first Americans to go up in an airplane. In 1910 the newly invented "flying machine" was little more than a kite, a fabulous toy regarded as not particularly safe. When Roosevelt, who was passing through St. Louis on a speaking tour, accepted Arch Hoxsey's invitation to go aloft, Missouri's Governor Hadley implored him not to risk his life. But the former Assistant Secretary of the Navy who had understood the significance of Langley's experiments and who later as President made possible the purchase of the first military airplane from the Wright brothers, was determined to try flying first hand. Wearing a borrowed cap, he grimly braced himself as the skeleton of wood, wire, and cloth roared into the air. The crowd held its breath as the plane circled the field twice and made a safe landing. The following year in a similar flight Hoxsey crashed and was killed.

111

SPORTSMAN

"The accident did not keep me in five minutes. I rode straight through the rest of the hunt. . . . I don't grudge the broken arm a bit. . . . I am always willing to pay the piper when I have had a good dance; and every now and then I like to drink the wine of life with brandy in it."
Letter to Henry Cabot Lodge

When it came to athletics, it would be difficult to find a non-professional as active or as proficient as was T.R. He was an excellent rider, and in his younger days played polo and rode to hounds. The broken arm, referred to in his letter to Lodge, occurred during a hunt when his horse failed to clear a five-foot fence. But riding was only the beginning of his athletic interests for he excelled in wrestling, canoeing, single stick, jiu-jitsu, swimming, rowing, and football. Boxing was one of his favorite sports, and he often had as sparring partner the middleweight champion of the United States. During one of these boxing sessions, when he was in the White House, his opponent hit him a sharp blow on the left eye, and soon afterward he lost the sight of the eye. Whether climbing the Matterhorn in his twenties or playing tennis in his fifties, he threw himself into every sport with an unflagging, youthful spirit.

YOUNG MAN'S HERO

"In life, as in a football game, the principle to follow is: hit the line hard; don't foul and don't shirk, but hit the line hard."

Reviewing the Boy Scouts at Oyster Bay.

T.R. had done everything of which a boy dreams. He was a fearless hunter, an intrepid explorer and an expert athlete; became President of the United States, and had even led a dashing cavalry charge. Little wonder that to the American boys of the day, Teddy Roosevelt was a veritable Frank Merriwell in the flesh. A boy at heart, he was warmly interested in young people, and made it his business to encourage them in all good things. Serving in the Boy Scout movement was only natural for a former national leader, but his active participation in the local Scout troop in Oyster Bay was characteristic of T.R. In the midst of a tumultuous life, he found pleasure in leading hikes, attending rallies, and greeting honor Scouts at his home. The words he spoke to them at their councils and campfires were the same cherished messages he gave to his own sons; the duties of uprightness, of manliness, of playing square, the privilege of being a free citizen. The proud lads who posed for his inspection on the lawn at Sagamore Hill instinctively knew that this fascinating and energetic man was the kind of American that every Boy Scout hopes someday to become.

115

Roosevelt unearths green turtle eggs while visiting the Louisia Wild Life Preserve which he had established when Preside

NATURALIST

"On some of the islands we found where green turtles had crawled up the beaches to bury their eggs in the sand. . . . One of them I dug up myself."

If Theodore Roosevelt had never entered public life, his accomplishments in the field of natural science would still have brought him into prominence. From the day in his boyhood when he acquired the head of a seal, his interest in the study of nature had broadened and deepened. No matter what geographical location was in question, he could name the trees, plants and flowers; the period of geological time of the rocks; and the English and Latin names of every bird, animal, and insect. It is impossible to say how he found time to expand his scientific knowledge and make significant contributions of his own as well. The first President to publish a book while in office, he wrote, not a treatise on government or politics, but instead on *The Deer Family*. He was an active member of several scientific societies, and numbered all of the leading naturalists of his day as his close friends. Known as an authority on the life histories and habits of big game animals, Roosevelt is regarded in scientific circles as one of the best field naturalists that the United States has produced.

PROGRESSIVE—1912

"A great democracy has got to be progressive, or it will soon cease to be either great or a democracy...."

Back home again as a private citizen after his travels, but with an enlarged world view, the Colonel was greatly disturbed by the conflict within his own party. The conservative block in Congress, silent when he was in office, now had the Roosevelt reforms under sharp attack. His successor, Taft, appeared to be siding with them, and T.R. feared that much of the work of his administration was in jeopardy. Moved by demands from the progressive wing of the party that he defend his policies, he announced his fateful decision to seek again the nation's highest office with the now famous phrase "My hat is in the ring." But the party bosses who once before had unsuccessfully tried to shelve him, were determined to keep Roosevelt out of office. With the Old Guard in control, the convention refused to seat large numbers of Roosevelt delegates, many of whom had been chosen in the new state primaries. When Taft was renominated on the first ballot the angry Roosevelt delegates left the hall to hold their own convention.

Roosevelt entering Chicago for the National Convention—1912

FOUNDER OF A NEW PARTY

The Bull Moose candidate addressing a street crowd during the presidential campaign.

"Our country—this great republic—means nothing unless it means the triumph of a real democracy, the triumph of popular government, and, in the long run, of an economic system under which each man shall be guaranteed the opportunity to show the best that there is in him."

The colorful convention which formed the National Progressive Party nominated Theodore Roosevelt for President, and his casual remark that he felt as fit as a bull moose gave the new party its familiar name. With the Republican party split, Roosevelt knew that he had but a slight chance to win against Wilson and Taft, but he could not turn his back on this latest battle in a war he had been waging for almost three decades. Now he believed that the Progressives, unfettered by reactionaries or party bosses, could immeasurably improve the lot of the common man, and strike a blow against the forces of special privilege that for so long had manipulated the government to serve their own ends. T.R. was at his best in a fight, and the almost irresistable appeal of his leadership drew about him some of the country's most forward-looking citizens. Many of the measures he championed, such as woman's suffrage, health insurance, workmen's compensation, and the income tax, which were regarded at the time as dangerously radical, are part of our national and state laws today.

121

ATTEMPTED ASSASSINATION

Roosevelt a few minutes after he was shot by a fanatic.

"I did not care a rap for being shot. It is a trade risk, which every prominent public man ought to accept as a matter of course."

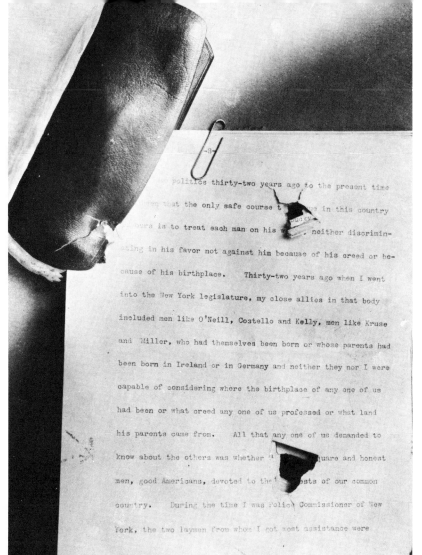

The bullet-pierced spectacle case and the speech that saved his life.

As the campaign of 1912 drew to a close, the attacks on Roosevelt increased in violence, and he was depicted as an ambitious politician grasping for personal power. Three weeks before the election, Roosevelt, emerging from his hotel in Milwaukee to make an important address, was shot in the chest by a fanatic. Pale and bleeding, he brushed aside the frantic pleas of his supporters, and went to the auditorium, declaring "I'll make this speech or die." Not until he had spoken the last word of his hour-and-a-half address would he consent to be examined. Doctors found that the bullet had broken a rib and barely missed his heart. The glasses case and folded speech in his breast-pocket had undoubtedly saved his life. The nation was electrified by his magnificent courage and only then did many realize his sincere and unselfish devotion to the Progressive cause. After a brief convalescence, Roosevelt made one last speech at Madison Square Garden. When the votes were counted he had beaten Taft, but Woodrow Wilson had won the election.

FAMILY PASTIMES

"There was not a vestige of breeze. . . . There was not the least shade. Because of the poison ivy we could not go near the trees. . . . Faces and necks were burned to a crisp. . . . In spite of it all, everybody considered that the picnic had been a great and glorious success."

Mrs. Theodore Roosevelt, Jr.

One of Roosevelt's joys was to find quiet and relaxation in the circle of his family at Sagamore Hill. During the long winter evenings in the drafty house, he was fond of reading in front of a roaring fire with Mrs. Roosevelt and the older children. But when summer came, he loved to spend the intervals between expeditions and political campaigns tramping the woods around Oyster Bay, and taking the family on outings. These often included long rows to a picnic site, and hours in the broiling sun. However, as his daughter-in-law, Mrs. Theodore Roosevelt, Jr., observed after her first Roosevelt picnic, distance and heat meant nothing to the indefatigable T.R. His boys regarded him as an ideal companion for an outdoor adventure. As one of his young admirers declared after a four-day hunting and sailing trip on the Great South Bay, "He never asked me to wash once."

JUNGLE EXPLORER

After his defeat in the campaign of 1912, and consequent retirement from politics, Roosevelt was restless for further adventure. He considered for a while a trip to the North Pole, but rejected this plan in favor of a geographic expedition into the Amazon jungle. Backed by the American Museum of Natural History and by the Brazilian Government, its object was to explore and chart the course of a large stream, the River of Doubt, which flowed into one of the most desolate areas on the face of the earth. Descending the river from its headwaters in Mato Grosso in primitive dugout canoes, the party nearly suffered complete disaster in the succession of rapids and falls which marked its entire course. Men, canoes, and supplies were lost in the white waters. Roosevelt, whose leg was injured trying to save a canoe, developed jungle fever. "This is not written very clearly; my temperature is 105," appears in the margin of his notes. With food supplies gone, the party barely managed to keep alive. After two months in the boats exploring a six-hundred-mile river never before seen by white men, the party reached an outpost of civilization. The river, which was found to be one of the major arms of the Amazon, was named "Rio Roosevelt" by the Brazilian Government.

"I had to go. It was my last chance to be a boy."

The Roosevelt expedition in the Amazon wilderness descending the River of Doubt.

V

THE FINAL

CAMPAIGN

"Life is a long campaign, where every victory merely leaves the ground free for another battle, and sooner or later defeat comes to every man, unless death forestalls it. But the final defeat does not and should not cancel the triumphs, if the latter have been substantial and for a cause worth championing."

Reviewing a war-time parade with Mayor Mitchel and Charles Evans Hughes from the steps of the New York Public Library.

THE GREAT WAR–
PREPAREDNESS

"For eighteen months, with this world-cyclone before our eyes, we as a nation have sat supine without preparing in any shape or way. . . . Such national short-sightedness, such national folly, is almost inconceivable."

His strength badly spent from the Brazilian ordeal, Roosevelt returned to what he supposed would be a quiet life at home. But in 1914 the world heard the rumblings in Sarajevo and overnight Europe was engulfed in war. Roosevelt knew the Kaiser's contempt for weakness, and recognized that United States' neutrality could only be preserved if its military forces were in good order. As German submarine warfare went into high gear, he strove to arouse the nation to its peril. To a people prosperous from the sale of supplies to the belligerents, he preached the duty of war to avenge America's humiliation on the high seas. Not until the sinking of the *Lusitania* did the country awake to Roosevelt's message.

Roosevelt attempts to rescue the sinking Allies.

In April 1917, the United States declared war on the Central Powers, but there were still few preparations being made to send American troops to support the fast-weakening Allies. One month after war was declared, Theodore Roosevelt offered to raise and lead a division of men, which he assured President Wilson would be trained and on the battlefront in France in ninety days. Preparations had been under way for some time; all officers had been selected and 250,000 men exempt from the draft had volunteered. Hard pressed by the German spring offensive, the leaders of France and England begged the President to send the Roosevelt Division as a symbol of American intervention. Wilson's note to Roosevelt informing him that his help would not be required was perhaps the greatest disappointment he had ever suffered. Turning his attention to the war on the home front, he served with the only means left to him—his voice and pen hammering incessantly for loyalty, unity, and above all, for the vigorous prosecution of the war. There are many who feel that this was his most unselfish service.

132

PATRIOT

May 18, 1917

To the President
White House
Washington, D. C.

I respectfully ask permission immediately to raise two divisions for immediate service at the front under the bill which has just become law, and hold myself ready to raise four divisions, if you so direct. . . .

Theodore Roosevelt

Twenty thousand men of the 84th Division at Camp Grant, Rockford, Illinois, listen to T.R. speak.

Quentin Roosevelt as a child at Sagamore Hill. (Killed in aerial combat over Germany, 1918, when he was 21 years old.

SACRIFICE

"Only those are fit to live who do not fear to die; and none are fit to die who have shrunk from the joy of life and the duty of life. Both life and death are part of the same Great Adventure."

Although T.R. was denied "the post of peril and honor," he was proud that his four sons were facing the enemy at the front. Two had trained as officers at Plattsburgh before the war, another served as an officer with the British Army in Mesopotamia, and the youngest was an aviator with the famous Ninety-fifth American Aero Squadron. All were with the first troops to arrive in France, and two were badly wounded. The youngest, Quentin, who but a few years before had been the leader of the White House Gang, was killed in an air battle behind the German lines. The words above, penned a few days later, were part of a patriotic father's tribute to his heroic son. Theodore Roosevelt would not live to know that two more of his sons, Kermit and Theodore, Jr., would also die in their country's service in the Second World War.

With his first grandch

GRANDFATHER

". . . it is the intimate and homely things that count most."

Although Theodore Roosevelt knew the pinnacle of fame, and dealt with the world's great, he never lost his enjoyment of the simpler things of life. While the young women, as well as the men of the family, were overseas, the grandchildren left behind at Sagamore Hill became his constant pleasure. In the sorrow of Quentin's death only the children had the power to make him happy. Few of those who heard his stirring speeches or read his countless editorials circulated nationally by the *Kansas City Star* realized that his health was failing rapidly. With the example of his patriotic service before them, Republicans and Progressives closed ranks in declaring him their next presidential candidate. On November 11, the day the Armistice was signed, Roosevelt entered the hospital seriously ill with inflammatory rheumatism. He had just passed his sixtieth birthday.

THE GREAT ADVENTURE

". . . serene and high of heart we must face our fate and go down into the darkness."

Borne to his grave at Oyster Bay.

He was home again at Sagamore Hill on Christmas, and had a wonderful day with his grandchildren. After the holidays, his health seemed to improve and he had hopes of resuming work at his old pace. On Sunday, January 5, 1919, feeling ill, he spent the day quietly in the sunny northwest bedroom, reading to Mrs. Roosevelt and chatting about the return of the family now that the war was over. He wrote a letter to his son Kermit, still overseas, and retired early. The next morning Theodore Roosevelt was dead.

EXEMPLAR OF AMERICAN IDEALS

"Far better it is to dare mighty things, to win glorious triumphs, even though checkered by failure, than to take rank with those poor spirits who neither enjoy much nor suffer much, because they live in the gray twilight that knows not victory nor defeat."

To a stunned America, it did not seem possible that the Niagara of energy that was Theodore Roosevelt had been stilled. One of the central characters in American politics for almost forty years, he had lived in an exciting and dramatic fashion, with accomplishments worthy of several lifetimes. Although he was a man of means who never needed to work for a livelihood, he took up the cause of the downtrodden; fought evil wherever he found it; preached and lived the "elemental virtues." Theodore Roosevelt was a valiant leader, a lover of all beauty in nature and in life, and an unforgettable personality. Something of what he was can be glimpsed in the recollections of a friend who described him as "one of the most astounding expressions of the Creative Spirit we had ever seen."

SOURCES

QUOTATIONS

Page 11: Speech before the Hamilton Club, Chicago, April 10, 1899
Page 13: *American Ideals* by Theodore Roosevelt; G. P. Putnam's Sons, New York
Page 15: *Theodore Roosevelt, An Autobiography;* Charles Scribner's Sons, New York
Pages 17, 18: *ibid*
Page 21: Letter to Richard Watson Gilder, August 20, 1903, from *Theodore Roosevelt and His Times,* by Joseph Buklin Bishop; Charles Scribner's Sons, New York
Page 22: Speech at Harvard commencement dinner, June 25, 1902
Page 25: *Theodore Roosevelt The Citizen* by Jacob A. Riis; The Macmillan Co., New York
Page 26: *Theodore Roosevelt, An Autobiography*
Page 29: Address as Assistant Secretary of the Navy before the Naval War College, June, 1897
Page 30: *Theodore Roosevelt* by Lord Charnwood; Atlantic Monthly Press, Boston
Page 33: Letter to Henry Cabot Lodge, October 10, 1891, *from Selections from the Correspondence of Theodore Roosevelt and Henry Cabot Lodge, 1884-1918;* Charles Scribner's Sons, New York
Page 34: Letter to Theodore Roosevelt, Jr., October 20, 1903, from *Letters of Theodore Roosevelt* by Elting Morison; Harvard University Press, Cambridge, Mass.
Page 37: Letter to Henry Cabot Lodge, June 29, 1889, from *Selections from the Correspondence of Theodore Roosevelt and Henry Cabot Lodge, 1884-1918;* Charles Scribner's Sons, New York
Page 39: *Theodore Roosevelt, An Autobiography*
Page 40: Speech at Groton School, Groton, Massachusetts, May 24, 1904
Page 43: *Theodore Roosevelt, An Autobiography*
Page 44: From the National Archives, Washington, D. C.
Page 47: *The Rough Riders* by Theodore Roosevelt; Charles Scribner's Sons, New York
Page 48: *ibid*
Page 50: Letter to General William R. Shafter, August 3, 1898, quoted in *The Rough Riders*
Page 53: Address at the Harvard Union, February 23, 1907
Page 54: Address at Colorado Springs, Colorado, August 2, 1901
Page 57: Letter to Henry Cabot Lodge, March 27, 1886, from *Selections from the Correspondence of Theodore Roosevelt and Henry Cabot Lodge, 1884-1918*
Page 58: *Theodore Roosevelt and His Times* by Joseph Buklin Bishop; Charles Scribner's Sons, New York
Page 61: Campaign speech, New York City, October 5, 1898
Page 62: Inaugural Address, March 4, 1905
Page 65: Speech at Osawatomie, Kansas, August 31, 1910
Page 67: *Theodore Roosevelt, An Autobiography*
Page 68: Speech at Carnegie Hall, New York, March 20, 1912
Page 69: *Letters to Kermit from Theodore Roosevelt,* edited by Will Erwin; Charles Scribner's Sons, New York
Page 73: Charter Day address, Berkeley, California, March 23, 1911
Page 74: Letter to E. S. Martin, November 6, 1908, from Bishop, *op. cit.*
Page 77: *Outdoor Pastimes of an American Hunter* by Theodore Roosevelt; Charles Scribner's Sons, New York
Page 79: Speech at Carnegie Hall, New York, March 20, 1912
Page 80: Address before the Nobel Peace Committee, Christiania, Norway, May 5, 1910
Page 83: Letter of November 19, 1905, from *Letters to Kermit from Theodore Roosevelt*
Page 85: Speech at Denver, Colorado, August 29, 1910
Page 86: *above,* Speech at Chicago, June 17, 1912
         below, American Ideals by Theodore Roosevelt
Page 87: Public letter to S. Stanwood Menken, January 10, 1917
Page 88: *Theodore Roosevelt, An Autobiography*
Page 91: Speech at the Minnesota State Fair, September 2, 1901
Page 92: Speech at Osawatomie, Kansas, August 31, 1910

Page 95: Speech at Carnegie Hall, New York, March 20, 1912
Page 97: *A Book-Lover's Holidays in the Open* by Theodore Roosevelt; Charles Scribner's Sons, New York
Page 98: *African Game Trails* by Theodore Roosevelt; Charles Scribner's Sons, New York
Page 101: Romanes Lecture, delivered at Oxford, England, June 7, 1910
Page 103: Letter to G. O. Trevalvan, October 1, 1911, quoted in Bishop, *op. cit.*
Page 104: Letter to P. Marcius Simons, March, 19, 1904, quoted in Bishop, *op. cit.*
Page 105: *Letters to Kermit from Theodore Roosevelt*
Page 106: Speech at the Battery, New York City, June 18, 1910
Page 109: Said of Theodore Roosevelt by his friend William Hard (in the *New Republic,* January 25, 1919)
Page 110: From the National Archives, Washington, D. C.
Page 112: Letter to Henry Cabot Lodge, October 30, 1885, quoted in *The Americanism of Theodore Roosevelt* by Hermann Hagedorn and J. A. Lester; Houghton Mifflin Co., Boston
Page 114: *Theodore Roosevelt The Citizen* by Jacob A. Riis; The Macmillan Co., New York
Page 117: *A Book-Lover's Holidays in the Open* by Theodore Roosevelt
Page 118: Speech before the Colorado Legislature, August 29, 1910
Page 121: Speech at Osawatomie, Kansas, August 31, 1910
Page 122: Letter to Sir Cecil Arthur Spring-Rice, December 31, 1912, from Bishop, *op. cit.*
Page 124: From "It All Comes Under the Head of Pleasure," an article by Mrs. Theodore Roosevelt, Jr. published in the *Delineator* and later quoted in *The Roosevelt Family of Sagamore Hill* by Hermann Hagedorn; The Macmillan Co., New York
Page 127: Lord Charnwood, *op. cit.*
Page 129: Letter to Sir George Otto Trevelyan, March 9, 1905, from Bishop, *op. cit.*
Page 131: *Fear God and Take Your Own Part* by Theodore Roosevelt; George H. Doran Co., New York
Page 133: Request to President Woodrow Wilson, 1917
Page 135: *The Great Adventure* by Theodore Roosevelt; Charles Scribner's Sons, New York
Page 137: *Theodore Roosevelt, An Autobiography*
Page 138: Bishop, *op. cit.*
Page 141: Speech before the Hamilton Club, Chicago, April 10, 1899

PHOTOGRAPHS

Photo on page 13: American Museum of Natural History

Photos on page 14: *above,* Harvard College Library; *below,* Theodore Roosevelt Association

Photo on page 16: Theodore Roosevelt Association

Photos on page 19: *above,* Harvard College Library; *below,* American Museum of Natural History

Photos on pages 20, 23: Harvard College Library

Photos on page 24: *above,* Arthur S. O'Neil, Ogdensburg, New York; *below,* Harvard College Library

Photo on page 27: Mrs. Theodore Roosevelt, Jr.

Photos on page 28: Harvard College Library

Photo on page 31: Brown Bros.; cartoon on same page: Shaw, Albert, *A Cartoon History of Roosevelt's Career,* Review of Reviews Co.

Photo on page 32: Mrs. Theodore Roosevelt, Jr.

Photos on pages 35, 36: Theodore Roosevelt Association

Photos on pages 38, 41; Harvard College Library

Photo on page 42: American Museum of Natural History

Photos on pages 44, 46, 49, 51: Harvard College Library

Photo on page 52: Theodore Roosevelt Association

Photos on pages 55, 56, 57, 59: Harvard College Library

Photo on page 61: Theodore Roosevelt Association

Photos on pages 63, 64: Harvard College Library

Photo on page 66: Theodore Roosevelt Association

Photo on page 67: Harvard College Library

Photos on page 68: Mrs. Richard Derby

Photos on pages 71, 72: Harvard College Library

Photo on page 74: The Submarine Library, Electric Boat Company, General Dynamics Corporation